P9-BYE-134

HILARIOUS Huge Animal JOKES to Tickle Your FUNNY BONE

Felicia Lowenstein Niven

Enslow Elementary

an imprint of

Enslow Publishers, Inc.

40 Industrial Road
Box 398
Berkeley Heights, NJ 07922
USA

http://www.enslow.com

Enslow Elementary, an imprint of Enslow Publishers, Inc.

Enslow Elementary® is a registered trademark of Enslow Publishers, Inc.

Library of Congress Cataloging-in-Publication Data

Niven, Felicia Lowenstein.

Hilarious huge animal jokes to tickle your funny bone / by Felicia Lowenstein Niven.

    pages cm — (Funniest bone animal jokes)

Includes index.

Summary: "Read jokes, limericks, tongue twisters, and knock-knock jokes about elephants and other large animals. Also find out fun facts about these animals"— Provided by publisher.

ISBN 978-0-7660-5948-1

1. Animals—Juvenile humor. I. Title.

PN6231.A5N58 2013

818'.602—dc23

2013009719

Future editions:
Paperback ISBN: 978-0-7660-5949-8
Single-User PDF ISBN: 978-0-7660-5951-1

EPUB ISBN: 978-0-7660-5950-4
Multi-User PDF ISBN: 978-0-7660-5952-8

Printed in the United States of America
072014 HF Group, North Manchester, IN
10 9 8 7 6 5 4 3 2 1

To Our Readers: We have done our best to make sure all Internet addresses in this book were active and appropriate when we went to press. However, the author and the publisher have no control over and assume no liability for the material available on those Internet sites or on other Web sites they may link to. Any comments or suggestions can be sent by e-mail to comments@enslow.com or to the address on the back cover.

Every effort has been made to locate all copyright holders of material used in this book. If any errors or omissions have occurred, corrections will be made in future editions of this book.

Illustration Credits: Clipart.com, pp. 6 (middle), 7 (top), 8 (bottom), 9 (top), 12 (top), 13 (middle, bottom), 14 (top), 20 (all), 23 (middle), 28 (middle), 29 (middle), 30 (bottom), 31 (top), 34 (middle, bottom), 36 (bottom), 38 (bottom), 39 (top), 41 (bottom), 43 (bottom); Shutterstock.com: Adrian Niederhaeuser, p. 6 (top); andryuha1981, p. 10 (bottom); Anikakodydkova, p. 19 (top); Anton Brand, p. 44 (bottom); Bannykh Alexey Vladimirovich, pp. 25 (middle), 33 (top); CABO, p. 38 (top); cupoftea, p. 5 (top); dedMazay, p. 44 (top); Gorban, p. 37; HitToon.Com, p. 19 (bottom); humphrey, p. 22 (bottom); Keanu, p. 15 (bottom); Ken Benner, p. 40 (top); Klara Viskova, pp. 23 (top), 41 (top); Kopirin, p. 13 (top); latino, p. 22 (middle); libdro, p. 25 (top); Liusa, p. 27 (bottom); Matthew Cole, pp. 7 (top), 23 (bottom), 29 (bottom); Otlan, p. 10 (top); Pushkin, pp. 4 (top), 11 (top), 12 (middle, bottom), 21 (top), 22 (top), 42 (top); Ron Leishman, p. 8 (top); Sarawut Padungkwan, p. 1; softRobot, p. 24 (bottom); steckfigures, p. 33 (bottom); Tatiana Ciumac, p. 30 (middle); Teguh Mujiono, p. 42 (bottom); Tim Carillet, p. 14 (bottom); totallyPic.com, p. 36 (middle); Virinaflora, p. 3 (all); Wimpos, p. 6 (bottom); Yayayoyo, p. 39 (bottom); YorkBerlin, p. 38 (middle); © Thinkstock: © Aleksandra Erkayeva/iStock, p. 25 (bottom); © Alexey Bannykh/Hemera, p. 40 (bottom); © Alexey Bannykh/iStock, pp. 32 (bottom), 35 (bottom); © Alisher Burhonov/iStock, p. 8 (middle); © Andrew Morrison/iStock, p. 30 (top); © Anton Brand/iStock, p. 11 (bottom); © Bob Ash/iStock, p. 26 (bottom); © Chatchai Nuchlamyong/iStock, p. 5 (middle); © dedMazay/iStock, pp. 26 (top), 29 (top); © Denis Voronin/iStock, p. 24 (middle); dicky_culle/Photos.com, p. 17 (bottom); © giraffarte/iStock, p. 18 (bottom); © Igor Zakowski/iStock, p. 32 (top); © Jana Guothova/iStock, p. 18 (middle); © John Hopkins/iStock, p. 9 (bottom); © Julien Tromeur/iStock, p. 17 (middle); © Klara Viskova/Hemera, p. 4 (bottom); © LLLozo/iStock, p. 16 (top); © maxicam/iStock, p. 31 (bottom); © Milorad Zaric/iStock, p. 16 (bottom); © natewidick/iStock, p. 34 (top); © Nikola Pavlovic/iStock, p. 17 (top); © plutofrosti/iStock, p. 36 (top); © Robert Harness/iStock, p. 35 (top); © Roland Netter/iStock, p. 43 (top); © rudall30/iStock, p. 27 (middle); © Sarah Knorr/iStock, p. 27 (top); © Valentin_Chemyakin/iStock, p. 15 (top); © vectorcartoons/iStock, p. 28 (top); © Vladimir Semenov/Hemera, p. 21 (bottom); © Vladislav Ociacia/iStock, p. 18 (top).

Cover Illustrations: Shutterstock.com: Yayayoyo (front), Pushkin (back).

Contents

① Fun With Elephants

What's big and gray and protects you from the rain?

An umbrellaphant!

The intelligence of elephants is irrelevant.

How do you stop an elephant from charging?

Take away its credit card.

What time is it when an elephant sits on your watch?

Time to get a new watch!

Patriotic pachyderms parade publicly.

What do you call an elephant in a compact car?

Stuck!

Why do elephants have trunks?

Because they don't have any pockets!

Knock, knock.

Who's there?

Olive.

Olive who?

Olive elephants, don't you?

DID YOU KNOW?

A male elephant is called a bull. A female is called a cow. And a baby elephant is called a calf.

How can you tell that an elephant is in the bathtub with you?

By the smell of peanuts on its breath.

Knock, knock.

Who's there?

Dumbo.

Dumbo who?

You don't recognize the famous flying elephant?

Limerick

Whatever you whisper, you can bet,
An elephant will never forget.
With a brilliant brain,
It easily retains
Your darkest secrets, without any sweat.

What do elephants have that nothing else has?

Baby elephants.

Limerick

When the latch on the gate I forgot,
Toward escape I saw elephants trot.
I looked high and low.
Just where did they go?
You'd think they'd be easier to spot.

Elephant

Mix-ups!

What do you get when you cross an elephant with a fish?

Swimming trunks!

What do you get when you cross an elephant and a whale?

Moby D. Elephant

Knock, knock.

Who's there?

Justin.

Justin who?

Justin time to feed the elephants!

FUN FACT

An elephant's eyes are fairly small compared to the rest of its body. It depends on senses other than its vision. In fact, a blind elephant has been known to lead a herd by using its trunk.

What do you get when you cross an elephant with a jaguar?

A car with a big trunk!

Take this tip: Don't trip on your trunk!

What do you get when you cross a Galapagos tortoise with a bad storm?

An I'm-not-in-a-hurry-cane!

What do you get when you cross an elephant with a skin doctor?

A pachydermatologist.

Dan was a fan of elephants.

What do you get when you cross a giant crocodile with a camera?

A snap-shot!

Knock, knock.

Who's there?

Luke.

Luke who?

Luke at all the elephants!

FUN FACT

Elephants have long eyelashes and a third eyelid. Both of these traits help protect the eye from sand, dust, and dirt.

The unlucky elephant Sam
Was stuck in a bit of a jam.
He had a big test,
And not enough rest,
So tonight he would just have to cram.

What do you get when you cross a giant ape with a dance step?

King Konga.

If you do not know what to wear,
An elephant can help you there.
The best look is gray,
And more is okay,
As long as you don't dye your hair!

3 Baby Elephants

How do you raise a baby elephant?

With a forklift!

What is a baby elephant's favorite vegetable?

Squash!

DID YOU KNOW?

A baby elephant weighs about 250 pounds at birth and stands 3 feet tall!

What do you call a baby elephant that never washes?

A smelly-phant!

Babbling baby elephants bring blankets, bibs, and big baby bottles.

Limerick

Baby elephants love splashing, they say.
In the water, they'll play and play.
But despite this great treat,
There's nothing that beats
Elephant hugs at the end of the day!

13

DID YOU KNOW?

Baby elephants will suck on their trunks, just like human babies suck their thumbs.

An elephant's trunk does it all.
It's like a long arm reaching tall.
It serves as a nose,
And wets like a hose.
They use it to drink or to call.

Seven silly elephants sit somewhere silently.

14

Knock, knock.

Who's there?

A herd.

A herd who?

A herd you were home so I came over.

Knock, knock.

Who's there?

Claire.

Claire who?

Claire the way; an elephant's coming through!

Why are baby elephants so wrinkled?

They take too long to iron!

What do you name a baby elephant hiding in a pile of leaves?

Russell.

Jungle Giants

Knock, knock.

Who's there?

Indy.

Indy who?

Indy jungle, the mighty jungle, the lion sleeps tonight.

What's the difference between an African rhino and an Indian rhino?

About 3,000 miles.

How do hippos travel?

In a hippopotabus.

DID YOU KNOW?

The largest elephant ever recorded was 13 feet tall and weighed about 24,000 pounds!

Limerick

The game that Crocodile likes to play
Is catch, and he plays it all day.
Here comes the ball
Right into his maw—
When you play, stay out of his way!

What large animal can put you in a trance?

A hipnopotamus.

Knock, knock.

Who's there?

Spy.

Spy who?

Spy-der!!!!

Jungle giraffes generally jiggle joyfully!

Limerick

**A long-necked giraffe named Pete
Was looking for something to eat.
The leaves he passed by,
The twigs he despised.
He opted instead for a sweet!**

FUN FACT

A giraffe can clean its own ears using its long tongue!

What do you call a hippo who says one thing but does something else?

A hippocrite.

Pippin the pop-eyed python pried pine nuts upside down.

Zoo Jokes

What kind of key opens a banana?

A monkey!

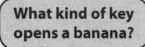

What do you get when you cross a giraffe and a hedgehog?

An extra long scrub brush!

Limerick

There once was a rhino named Dwight.
Who traveled much faster than light.
He set out one day
In the usual way
And got home the previous night!

FUN FACT

Rhinos make their own sunblock. They just roll in the mud and let it dry. Not only does it protect them from the sun, it keeps away bloodsucking insects, too!

If a dictionary goes from A to Z, what goes from Z to A?

A zebra!

Why do gorillas have big nostrils?

They have big fingers!

Knock, knock.

Who's there?

Needle.

Needle who?

Needle-nother ticket for the zoo!

What is black and white and black and white and black and white?

A zebra stuck in a revolving door!

DID YOU KNOW?

Elephants sleep standing up. They do not have to lie down because of the excellent support they get from their strong legs.

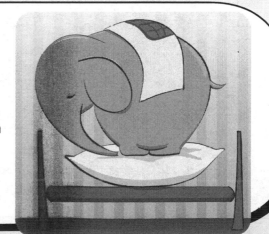

Orangutan Dan, in search of a meal,
Spied some fruit in a bowl of oatmeal.
"I'm not sure I'll eat
The cereal—too sweet—
But the banana has real appeal!"

What did the orangutan call his first wife?

His prime mate!

Knock, knock.

Who's there?

Noah.

Noah who?

Noah good zoo around here?

Tammy tangled with a temperamental orangutan.

What do you get when two giraffes collide?

A giraffic jam!

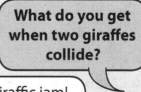

There's not much to manage in an imaginary menagerie.

What's worse than a giraffe with a **sore** throat?

A centipede with athlete's foot!

Why do giraffes have such long necks?

So they don't have to smell their feet!

Knock, knock.

Who's there?

CD.

CD who?

CD giraffe up there? He sees you!

What do you get when **giraffes** take over **your playground?**

Giraffic Park.

Why aren't there any giraffes in elementary school?

Because they are all in high school!

6 The Peanut Gallery

What do you call a peanut in a spacesuit?

An astro-nut!

Which is stronger: an elephant or a snail?

A snail because it can carry its own house; an elephant just carries a trunk!

DID YOU KNOW?

Elephants really don't like peanuts that much. They do not eat them in the wild, even though peanuts grow in some of their habitats. Captive elephants don't show much interest in peanuts either. That they ever did is a mysterious myth.

What is the biggest ant in the world?

An eleph-ANT!

Puny Peter picked plenty of peanuts.

Mousy mice make merry merrily.

Knock, knock.

Who's there?

Mice go.

Mice go who?

Mice don't go "who," they go "squeak"!

What do you call a mouse that can pick up an elephant?

Sir.

25

FUN FACT

Are elephants *really* afraid of mice? No. That's just a rumor that started because an elephant will move away when it sees a mouse. If the elephant is afraid, it's probably only because it might step on it!

Knock, knock.

Who's there?

Warren.

Warren who?

Warrening: Elephant coming through!

Limerick

The mouse in the house was so fat,
Left a dent wherever he sat.
That's how the cat knew
To look for the clue,
And that was the end of that.

"Time for dinner," the ant mama said
To her babies, who were always well fed.
"Are bread crumbs all right?"
The babes wouldn't bite.
"Let's call out for pizza instead."

Why do ducks have flat feet?

For stamping out forest fires.

Why do elephants have flat feet?

For stamping out flaming ducks!

What is gray and has four legs and a trunk?

A mouse going on vacation.

What is brown and has four legs and a trunk?

A mouse coming back from vacation.

7 Big, Bigger, Biggest

What was the Galapagos tortoise doing on the highway?

About 100 millimeters per hour.

Knock, knock.

Who's there?

Scold.

Scold who?

Scold enough out here for polar bears!

DID YOU KNOW?

Elephants are some of the most intelligent animals. They have a brain that, compared with the size of their body, is larger than any other land animal.

What do you call an alligator that has your mother's sister for dinner?

An aunt-eater!

What's an alligator's favorite drink?

Gator-ade.

What do you call a camel with no humps?

Humphrey (Hump-free)!

Limerick

The polar bear sniffed the igloo.
For his winter nap, it would do.
But first for a snack—
Oh, the people are back!
I'd say that dreams sometimes come true!

Limerick

A camel with one hump, not two,
Gave kids a ride at the zoo.
The kids would climb up
And then say, "Hup, hup!"
And they'd stick to his hump like glue.

Where do polar bears go to dance?

Snowballs!

What do you call reptiles that lurk between tall buildings?

Alley-gators.

What do you call a sick alligator?

An illigator.

FUN FACT

Goliath bird-eating spiders are the largest spiders in the world. Their leg span is 10 inches, nearly the length of a ruler! Don't worry about running into one, though. They live deep in the rain forests of South America.

What do giant pandas wear when they're robbing a bank?

A pandana!

Carry on, it's camel camaraderie!

What's white, furry, and throws snowballs?

A bowler bear!

Prepare for panda pandemonium!

8 Giants of the Sea

Knock, knock.

Who's there?

Alex.

Alex who?

Alex plain about the walrus in the bathtub later!

How do you cut the sea in half?

With a giant sea saw!

Where do giant sea creatures go to see the movies?

The dive-in!

DID YOU KNOW?

The blue whale is the largest known mammal. It can be up to 105 feet long and weigh 150 tons. That is about the weight of 150 small cars!

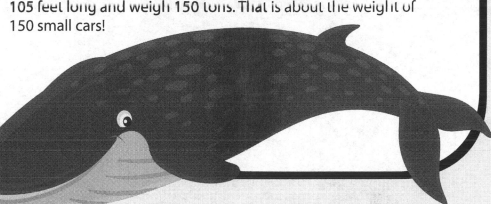

How do you make a whale float?

With root beer and ice cream!

Why does the walrus swim in salt water?

Because pepper makes him sneeze!

Why did the dolphin cross the ocean?

To get to the other tide!

Wily Willy the Whale wanders wearily through the waves.

What do whales like to chew?

Blubber gum!

Limerick
**There's nothing as big as the sea.
Its creatures are pleased as can be.
The temp is just right
For a swim day or night.
Just try it; we think you'll agree.**

Where do killer whales go to get braces?

The orca-dontist!

FUN FACT

A walrus can remain under water for up to 30 minutes before coming up for air.

Limerick

There once was a silly old whale
Who liked to chase his own tail.
One day he missed,
And got in a twist,
And had to get help from a snail.

Sneaky sharks slink through the salty sea.

Knock, knock.

Who's there?

Harry.

Harry who?

Harry up! There's a killer whale after us!

9 Prehistoric Humor

What do you get when dinosaurs crash?

Tyrannosaurus wrecks!

Where does a triceratops sit?

On its tricera-bottom!

What do you call a fossil that doesn't want to work?

Lazy bones!

DID YOU KNOW?

The word *dinosaur* comes from the Greek language. It means "terrible lizard."

Limerick

Dinosaurs ruled the earth long ago.
Their size made them fearsome, I know.
Today we see 'em
In a big museum
And can only imagine the show.

Knock, knock.

Who's there?

Ty.

Ty who?

Tyrannosaurus rex.
You better run!

How do you know if a dinosaur is in bed with you?

By the dino-snores!

What do you call a dinosaur that never gives up?

Try-try-try-ceratops.

Where did prehistoric reptiles go on vacation?

To the dino-shore!

Knock, knock.

Who's there?

Dino.

Dino who?

Dinosaur!

The dinosaur's dinner delighted the *Dilophosaurus*.

Limerick

Apatosaurus is a scary beast.
Up close his fearsomeness will increase.
You might shake in fear,
When he comes near,
But don't worry—plants are his feast.

FUN FACT

Most dinosaurs ate plants instead of other animals.

What do you get when you cross a dinosaur with fireworks?

Dino-mite!

What do you say when you meet a two-headed dinosaur?

"Hello, hello."

How do dinosaurs pay their bills?

With Tyrannosaurus checks!

Don't tangle with a tyrannical pterodactyl!

10 Hugely Funny!

Why can't you find a good animal doctor?

Because animals have a hard time getting into medical school!

A pack of pretty pachyderms pranced in the park after dark.

Limerick

A walrus who came from Debusk
Thought he had the handsomest tusks.
To attract the ladies
He'd chuff and he'd sneeze
And wear tons of his smelliest musk.

DID YOU KNOW?

An elephant uses its trunk like a snorkel when it swims in deep water.

African, Asian, and Indian elephants amble aimlessly.

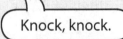

Knock, knock.

Who's there?

Elephant.

Hey, you smashed my door!

Sorry.

What is an elephant's favorite sport?

Squash!

What came after the elephant?

Its tail!

Knock, knock.

Who's there?

Canoe.

Canoe who?

Canoe help me? I need to move an elephant out of my vegetable garden!

How do you hide an elephant in a strawberry patch?

You paint its toenails red.

43

What's the biggest moth in the world?

A mammoth!

What's as big as an elephant but weighs nothing?

An elephant's shadow.

Limerick

There once was an elephant roar
That could clearly be heard next door.
Said neighbor to friend,
"This isn't the end.
Just wait until we start to snore!"

Make a Big Animal Cartoon

HERE'S WHAT YOU WILL NEED:

- a joke book
- a piece of white paper
- a pencil and markers or crayons
- a ruler

DIRECTIONS:

1. Use a ruler and the pencil to draw two large squares side by side on your paper.

2. Choose one of the jokes in this book to illustrate.

3. Write the beginning part of the joke at the top of the first square, leaving plenty of space for a picture.

4. Write the punch line in the second square, also leaving plenty of room for a picture.

5. Now draw pictures to show what is happening in each square. For example:

   What's big and gray and protects you from the rain? (picture of rain or kids getting wet)

   An umbrellaphant! (an elephant that has an umbrella as part of its head)

6. Color your cartoon, and don't forget to sign your name. After all, you are the artist!

Words to Know

fossil—The remains of a once-living prehistoric thing left in rock or another substance.

joke—Something said to make people laugh.

limerick—A funny five-line poem in which the first, second, and fifth lines rhyme, and the shorter third and fourth lines rhyme.

mammal—Any of the warm-blooded animals with a covering of hair and whose females produce milk to feed their young.

musk—A strong odor that many animals naturally have.

orca—A small, black-and-white toothed whale; it is also called a killer whale.

pachyderm—A large mammal with hooves or nails that look like hooves and usually thick skin, such as an elephant, rhinoceros, or hippopotamus.

pandemonium—A noisy uproar.

prehistoric—Being from the time before the invention of writing and recorded history.

primate—A type of mammal with flexible hands and feet and a highly developed brain.

pterodactyl—Any of the extinct flying reptiles that lived in prehistoric times.

tongue twister—A series of fun words with similar sounds that can be hard to say out loud.

Read More

Books

Dahl, Michael. *The Funny Farm: Jokes About Dogs, Cats, Ducks, Snakes, Bears and Other Animals*. North Mankato, Minn.: Picture Window Books, 2010.

Elliott, Rob. *Zoolarious Animal Jokes for Kids*. Ada, Mich.: Revell, 2012.

Lederer, Richard, and Jim Ertner. *Super Funny Animal Jokes*. Portland, Oreg.: Marion Street Press, 2011.

National Geographic Kids Just Joking: 300 Hilarious Jokes, Tricky Tongue Twisters, and Ridiculous Riddles. New York: National Geographic Children's Books, 2012.

Internet Addresses

National Geographic Kids: Animals: Creature Features: Polar Bears
http://kids.nationalgeographic.com/kids/animals/creaturefeature/polar-bear/

San Diego Zoo Animals: Whale
http://animals.sandiegozoo.org/animals/whale

Smithsonian National Zoological Park: Asian Elephants
http://nationalzoo.si.edu/Animals/AsianElephants/

Index